BODIES IN

CRISIS

NUTRITIONAL
D I S E A S E S

Jon Zonderman and Laurel Shader, M.D.

Twenty-First Century Books

A Division of Henry Holt and Company
New York

Twenty-First Century Books
A Division of Henry Holt and Company, Inc.
115 West 18th Street
New York, New York 10011

Henry Holt® and colophon are trademarks of Henry Holt and
Company, Inc.
Publishers since 1866

Published in Canada by Fitzhenry & Whiteside Ltd.
195 Allstate Parkway, Markham, Ontario L3R 4T8

Printed in Mexico
All first editions are printed on acid-free paper ∞.

Created and produced in association with Blackbirch Graphics, Inc.

Library of Congress Cataloging-in-Publication Data

Zonderman, Jon.
    Nutritional diseases / Jon Zonderman and Laurel Shader, M.D. — 1st. ed.
       p.   cm. — (Bodies in crisis)
    Includes bibliographical references and index.
    Summary: Discusses a variety of topics related to diet and disease, including
malnutrition, eating disorders, digestive diseases, and food allergies.
    ISBN 0-8050-2601-0 (acid-free paper)
    1. Nutritionally induced diseases—Juvenile literature. [1. Nutritionally induced
diseases. 2. Diseases.] I. Shader, Laurel. II. Title. III. Series.
    RC622.Z65 1993
    616.3'9—dc20
                                                                                    93-25914
                                                                                     CIP
                                                                                     MG

Contents

Proteins, fats, carbohydrates, fiber, vitamins, minerals, and water are all essential nutrients. Including all of these nutrients in a balanced diet will help ensure the healthy development of the mind and body.

1

Good Nutrition and Malnutrition

Good nutrition, or eating right, is one of the keys to health and well-being. Following the proper diet, having clean water to drink, and getting enough rest and exercise are essential for growth, health, and normal physical and mental development. Malnutrition—not having a properly balanced diet—can leave the body open to a host of problems.

In many parts of the world, diet is not a topic of discussion—you eat whatever is available. But when many foods are available, and when people can afford to buy them, foods should be combined in the right way to provide our bodies with the needed nutrients (substances such as proteins, minerals, and vitamins).

As recently as 30 years ago, the focus of nutritional research in the United States was on the problem of lack of proper food and the diseases resulting from poor nutrition. Today, the major nutritional problem is the consumption of too much food, especially those foods containing a lot of fats and sugars. Despite this, malnutrition has not been completely eliminated—pockets of malnutrition exist especially among the rural and inner-city poor and the elderly.

Food Groups and the Essential Nutrients

All foods fall into one of 5 food groups: milk, meat, vegetable, fruit, and grain. Another category, called "other," includes fats, oils, and sweets. The chart on pages 14–15 lists the foods in these groups along with the daily servings that are recommended for maintaining a balanced diet.

Within all foods are found at least some of the 7 essential nutrients. Different food groups have various amounts of these nutrients: proteins, carbohydrates, fats, fiber, vitamins, minerals, and water.

Proteins are the main structural components of tissues and organs. They are needed for growth and cell repair. The building blocks of proteins are amino acids, 12 of which are produced naturally in our bodies, and 8 of which we take in through food. High concentrations of "essential amino acids"—the ones we must get from food—are found in meats (beef, chicken, turkey, lamb, and pork), as well as in eggs, milk, and cheese. Fewer amino acids are found in grains or vegetables.

Because of this, vegetarians (people who don't eat meat) must either eat a lot of eggs, milk, and cheese or,

Carbohydrates—compounds made up of carbon, hydrogen, and oxygen—are found in fruits, grains, and vegetables. Carbohydrates are produced by green plants in the process of photosynthesis (the process by which green plants make food).

Combining various plant proteins (vegetables and grains) over the course of a day is a sufficient means of supplying the body with the daily necessary requirements of essential amino acids.

if they don't eat any animal products, must eat even more of such grains as rice, wheat, and corn, and such vegetables as peas and beans.

Carbohydrates are starches and sugars and are found primarily in grains, fruits, and vegetables. The starches, or complex carbohydrates, are found mostly in grains and leafy green vegetables, such as spinach, broccoli, and lettuce. The sugars, or simple carbohydrates, are found in all fruits and vegetables, as well as in refined, or processed, sugars, which are made mostly from beets, sugarcane (sucrose), or corn syrup (fructose). The unrefined carbohydrates of cereals and fruits generally contain more fiber and nutrients than refined carbohydrates. Carbohydrates are the main sources of energy necessary for metabolism (the chemical processes that take place in the body, such as digesting food, eliminating wastes, and breathing).

Fats, along with proteins and carbohydrates, supply energy to the body. They also help the body absorb certain vitamins. Small amounts of fat are necessary for normal body functions.

Fats are found in the tissues of animals and plants, especially in the seeds of plants. They can be hard (like the fat of beef), soft (like butter), or liquid (like corn oil).

All fatty foods are made up of a combination of fatty acids. Fatty acids are probably best known for their relationship to heart disease, through the mechanism of blood cholesterol. Cholesterol is a soft, waxy substance that circulates in the blood and is important for general health. Since the body makes its own cholesterol, we don't need to get much from the foods we eat. Diets that are rich in foods containing cholesterol—egg yolks, fatty meats, and butter, for example—can often make the blood cholesterol level dangerously high. Excess blood cholesterol narrows the coronary arteries (arteries that supply oxygen and nutrients directly to the heart muscle), slowing down the flow of blood. A fatal heart attack can result.

Fiber is a material in plants that cannot be digested. It thus passes through the intestine unchanged. Nonetheless, fiber is essential to a healthful diet. A diet low in

In addition to providing the body with good nutrients, it is important to maintain an active lifestyle. Exercise develops muscles, promotes flexibility, and is essential for overall health.

fiber can cause constipation and other intestinal problems. Also, since a low-fiber diet is generally high in refined carbohydrates and fats, it can lead to obesity (overweight) and heart disease. A high-fiber diet, one that includes lots of raw vegetables, fruits, grains, and cereals, provides bulk and helps to keep body weight at a healthful level.

Vitamins help the body process proteins, carbohydrates, and fats, ensuring the healthy functioning of the brain, nerves, muscles, bones, and skin. Some vitamins also help in the production of blood cells, hormones, genetic material, and other body chemicals. All of the 13 essential vitamins are required by the body in small amounts. They are broken into two groups: fat-soluble vitamins and water-soluble vitamins.

Minerals are generally provided in sufficient quantity by a balanced diet. A few essential minerals are needed in large quantities by the body: Calcium, phosphorus, and magnesium are necessary for healthy bones and teeth, potassium is needed for muscle development, iron is needed for red blood cell formation and the transport of oxygen, sodium (salt) regulates body fluids, and sulfur plays an important role in the formation of bones, tendons, connective tissue and in the health of the hair, skin, and nails.

The body also needs a host of so-called micro minerals in much smaller quantities. Among them are iodine, zinc, copper, fluoride, and manganese. Minerals come from foods such as meats, fish, grains, beans, iodized salt, and also from fluoridated water.

Water is the most important element in life, and a large amount of clean water is necessary every day for good nutrition. It helps the body digest food, process waste, regulate body temperature, and circulate blood. While the body can survive on water alone, the other essential nutrients are fundamental to maintain a strong and healthy body.

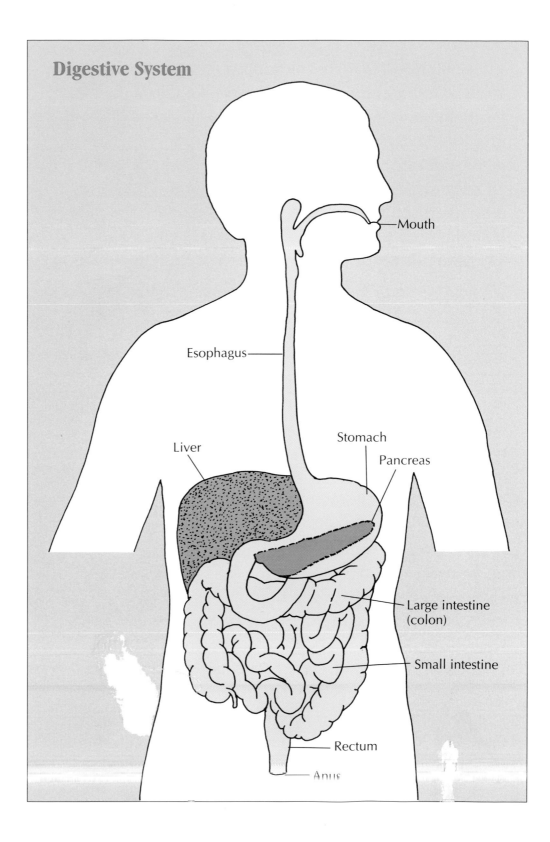

Digestive System

Mouth

Esophagus

Liver

Stomach

Pancreas

Large intestine (colon)

Small intestine

Rectum

Anus

How the Body Uses Nutrients

Think of the body as a machine, and food as fuel. The body needs this energy to stay active and healthy. We measure the amount of "fuel" contained in a given food by the number of calories it contains. A calorie is the amount of energy or heat it takes to raise 1 gram (0.6 pound) of water 1 degree centigrade (1.8 degrees Fahrenheit). The body breaks down substances into their simplest form—simple carbohydrates—to use them as calories for energy.

Just as different foods contain different essential nutrients, they also contain different amounts of fuel, also known as the caloric value. Each one of us needs a different total caloric intake for our body to function properly. Men need more than women; teens need more than adults; tall or large-boned people need more than short and small-boned people.

Digestion begins when food is chewed or swallowed and mixed with saliva. This process continues in the stomach, and absorption of the essential nutrients takes place in the small intestine.

Proper nutrition can be as simple as eating a good variety of foods. For example, a typical teenage girl, who should take in about 2,200 calories a day, or a typical teenage boy, who should take in about 2,800 calories a day, should get their daily intake in about the proportions indicated in the chart on pages 14–15.

Protein-containing tissues—including muscles and internal organs—should make up about 50 to 60 percent of your total body weight. Add bones and water, and

Good
Nutrition and
Malnutrition

13

The Five Food Groups

It's easy to eat the foods you need to be healthy. Just follow these two basic rules:

1. *Eat foods from each of the five food groups every day.* Each one of these groups provides you with the different essential nutrients that you need.

2. *Choose different foods from each group every day.* In every food group there are some foods that are better sources of a nutrient than others. By changing the foods you eat from each food group on a daily basis, you will get more of the nutrients you need.

INCLUDE IN YOUR DAILY DIET:	SUGGESTED SERVING SIZES

Milk Group

for calcium

2–4 servings

| Milk 1 cup | Cheese 1 1/2–2 oz. | Ice cream, ice milk, frozen yogurt 1/2 cup | Yogurt 1 cup | Cottage cheese 1/2 cup |

Meat Group

for iron

2–3 servings

| Cooked, lean poultry, fish 2–3 oz. | Cooked, lean meat 2–3 oz. | Cooked, dried peas, dried beans 1/2 cup | Peanut butter 2 tbsp. | Egg 1 |

Vegetable Group

for vitamin A

3–5 servings

| Raw vegetable 1/2 cup | Raw leafy vegetable 1 cup | Potato 1 medium | Cooked vegetable 1/2 cup | Juice 3/4 cup |

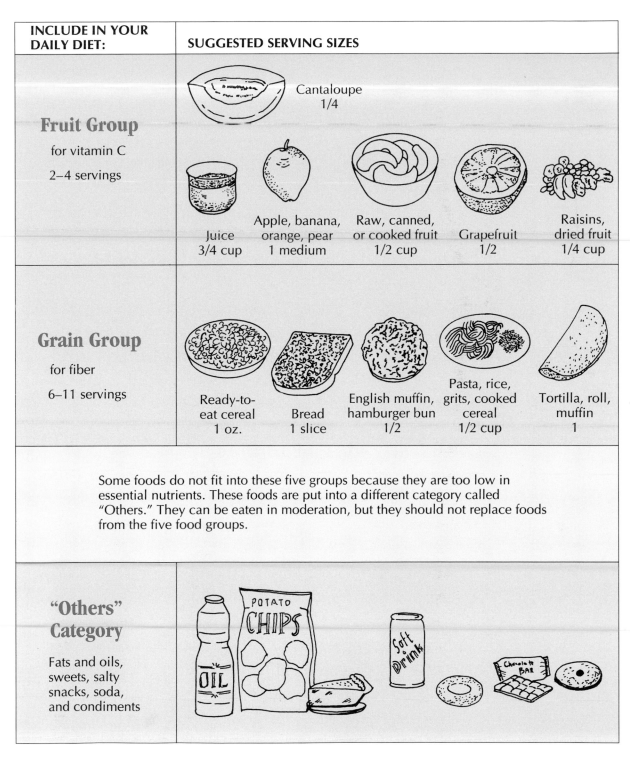

INCLUDE IN YOUR DAILY DIET:	SUGGESTED SERVING SIZES
Fruit Group for vitamin C 2–4 servings	Cantaloupe 1/4 Juice 3/4 cup — Apple, banana, orange, pear 1 medium — Raw, canned, or cooked fruit 1/2 cup — Grapefruit 1/2 — Raisins, dried fruit 1/4 cup
Grain Group for fiber 6–11 servings	Ready-to-eat cereal 1 oz. — Bread 1 slice — English muffin, hamburger bun 1/2 — Pasta, rice, grits, cooked cereal 1/2 cup — Tortilla, roll, muffin 1

Some foods do not fit into these five groups because they are too low in essential nutrients. These foods are put into a different category called "Others." They can be eaten in moderation, but they should not replace foods from the five food groups.

"Others" Category Fats and oils, sweets, salty snacks, soda, and condiments	

the proportion of body weight that is fat should be less than 20 percent (athletes such as marathon runners often have body fat content of less than 10 percent.)

One of the goals of good nutrition is to take in calories in their most efficient form. Proteins must be broken down into fats, and then into carbohydrates in order to be used as energy. Fats must also be broken down. Only enough of these nutrients should be included in the diet to bring in the necessary vitamin and mineral content and to maintain the right proportions of your total body weight.

The rest of the diet should be in the form of complex carbohydrates as much as possible. Most simple carbohydrates—including all refined sugars—are so-called empty calories because they provide caloric content without real nutritional value.

Watch Out for Malnutrition

Malnutrition can occur for a number of reasons. Eating disorders such as anorexia nervosa, in which people purposely starve themselves, or bulimia nervosa, in which people eat too much and then make themselves vomit before they can digest, are most common among teenagers, when body image is an important component of self-image. The opposite disorder, obesity, is caused when people eat more than their body can effectively use for energy. These eating disorders are discussed in detail in Chapter 2.

Digestive diseases, the subject of Chapter 3, can also cause malnutrition. A variety of infections of the gastrointestinal tract—those that affect the stomach and the intestines—can keep one from eating or digesting food properly until they are treated. A condition called short-gut syndrome—which can be either a problem from birth or the result of surgical removal of part of the small intestine because of accident or disease—causes poor absorption or nonabsorption of some nutrients. Crohn's disease, an inflammatory bowel disease, also often affects the small intestine, damaging the tissue so that it cannot absorb nutrients. Ulcerative colitis, another inflammatory bowel disease, can cause the body to lose essential fluids through watery bowel movements.

Alcohol and drug abuse lead to malnutrition, too. Alcoholic beverages are empty calories—fermented grain. Fermentation breaks down complex carbohydrates into simple carbohydrates. Those who drink excessively often "drink their lunch" or "drink their supper," taking in a full meal's worth of calories that have no nutritional content.

In addition, alcohol suppresses the small intestine's ability to absorb the essential nutrients thiamine and folic acid. Also, alcohol is toxic to the liver and injures its cells, causing them to inflame and hindering their function. In this expanded state they take on the appearance of fat cells. This condition is known as "fatty liver."

Some drugs, such as amphetamines or caffeine, suppress the appetite and are sold as "diet pills." Cocaine and the opiate drugs, such as codeine and heroin, slow the muscular contractions of the digestive tract and can cause people to lose all interest in eating.

Self-induced vomiting is a common symptom of bulimia nervosa. Bulimia nervosa—one of several eating disorders that can cause severe medical complications—is found mainly in young women and is associated with a lack of self-esteem.

2

Eating Disorders

Every year, millions of people in the United States develop very serious eating disorders. According to the National Institutes of Health, more than 90 percent of these people are teenagers and young women. In this chapter, obesity, anorexia nervosa, bulimia nervosa, and binge eating disorder—all major eating disorders—will be discussed. Each of these disorders has many contributing factors, and each is responsible for a wide variety of health problems.

Obesity
Obesity is described as a condition of excessive weight, occurring when the body's intake of energy (calories) surpasses its need. This results in the storage of the excess energy in the form of fat.

The American Medical Association estimates that about 25 percent of Americans are overweight and that 5 to 10 percent of all children in the United States are overweight. Between 13 and 23 percent of teenagers—especially girls—are obese, and 80 percent of them are likely to remain obese as adults.

Sometimes obesity is caused by illnesses involving the central nervous system or the endocrine system, which regulates the body's hormones. It can be a side effect of certain medications, and it can also be caused by defective genes (the elements of cells that determine characteristics and that are passed on by parents).

Most often, however, obesity in young children is simply caused by overeating. Also, children who have one obese parent are more likely to become obese than children whose parents are of normal weight. The earlier a child's weight problem is recognized and treated, the more likely it is that the problem can be remedied. Obese adolescents, on the other hand, are at increased risk of having lifelong problems with their weight and their health.

There are a number of physical and mental problems associated with obesity. Obese adolescents and adults are most likely to be affected by the complications of their excessive weight, including such problems as high blood pressure, diabetes, stress on bones and joints, and breathing difficulties. Many obese children and adolescents also suffer from poor self-esteem. They are often discriminated against and teased, and they can be a tremendous source of stress within their families.

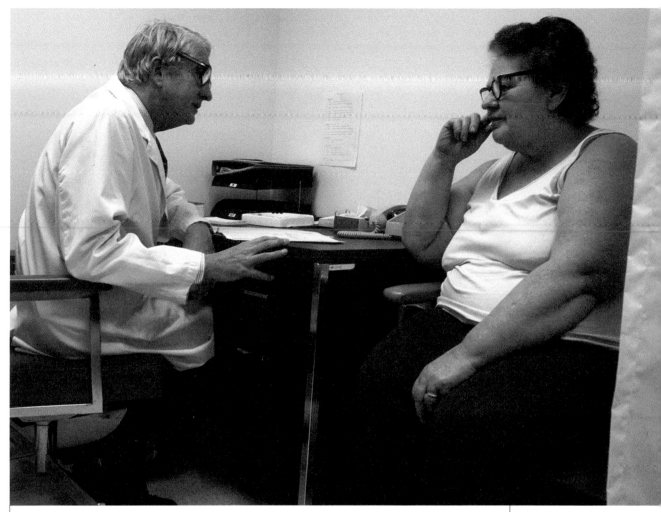

In extreme cases of adult obesity, a surgical procedure is used that allows food to bypass the stomach or small intestine so that fewer calories are absorbed. Sometimes the jaw is also wired so that meals can be taken in liquid form only through a straw. The ideal treatment for obesity, however, is slow and controlled weight loss through a combination of reduced food intake and proper exercise, along with a program of psychological support.

An obese patient consults with her physician about controlling her weight. Seeking medical advice is important for obese people because obesity can lead to other health problems.

Anorexia Nervosa

Anorexia nervosa is an eating disorder characterized by excessive weight loss. Its victims weigh about 15 percent below their normal body weight. People become anorexic through a combination of factors: by refusing to eat, by overexercising, and occasionally by deliberately vomiting and using laxatives (medication to increase a patient's number of bowel movements).

Anorexia is seen much more often in girls than in boys; in fact, it is rare in boys. It can begin as early as age 13 or 14 and sometimes appears after age 25. Usually, however, it begins in girls between the ages of 16 and 18. The condition is not common and is seen in about 1 percent of girls in this age group.

People suffering from anorexia have a distorted image of their own body. They believe that they are fat even when, in fact, they are dangerously thin. Anorexia is most often found in intelligent, compulsive, "good" girls who also have poor self-esteem. It is believed that many girls develop anorexia as a way of rebelling against their families and delaying the onset of puberty (the time when the body becomes sexually mature).

Anorexia causes damage to most of the body's systems as a result of extreme malnutrition. The major problems are bradycardia (abnormally slow heart rate) and hypotension (low blood pressure), which can result in death from heart failure. Sleep disturbances, hypothermia (low body temperature), constipation, and amenorrhea (lack of monthly menstrual periods) are also common problems among anorexics.

Numerous weight-control products are readily available in most drugstores and supermarkets. Many of these products can endanger health if they are misused.

Anorexia is most successfully treated when diagnosed early. It is sometimes difficult, however, to get people to admit they have a problem. Parents and teachers can talk with the victims to try to encourage them to seek treatment and counseling. The longer the problem continues, the more difficult it is for the person to overcome the problem and the toll it takes on the body.

Bulimia Nervosa

Bulimia nervosa, defined as alternating binges of eating and purging (self-induced vomiting) can exist as a separate eating disorder or can occur in cycles with anorexia. Bulimia is more common than anorexia and is seen in approximately 10 to 20 percent of adolescent girls and young women and far less frequently among teenage boys and young men.

Unlike anorexics, who resist eating, bulimics intermittently eat large amounts of high-calorie foods. They then purge themselves by forcing themselves to vomit, exercising excessively, abusing laxatives, and taking enemas. Since most people who suffer from bulimia tend to binge and purge in secret and are not skinny, they are often able to hide their problem from others.

The common complications of bulimia are similar to those of anorexia. Other associated problems include esophagitis (inflammation of the esophagus) and dental cavities, both of which are caused by exposing the esophagus and mouth to partially digested foods and stomach acids.

A Teenage Anorexic

Sixteen-year-old Heather Nelson (not her real name) was a shy young girl, a good student, and a people-pleaser. She was also pretty, but she was a little overweight. This bothered Heather. She thought that boys would not be interested in her unless she was thin.

One day, her father, in a joking way, commented that she'd probably never get a date unless she lost weight. This convinced Heather that she was indeed too fat, so she started dieting rigorously. She kept getting thinner and thinner, but when she looked in the mirror, she continued to see a fat Heather.

As her anorexia progressed, Heather became increasingly obsessed with food and losing weight, and she developed some odd eating rituals. Each day, she would weigh her daily ration of food on a kitchen scale, cut up the solids into very tiny pieces, and then place the food in containers, which she'd neatly line up. In addition, she would exercise to the point of exhaustion and refused to take an elevator if there were stairs. Outwardly she looked sick because she was so skinny, and the anorexia had also affected the functioning of her body to the extent that she no longer had her monthly periods.

Everyone who saw Heather knew she had a problem, but no one was able to convince her of that. Heather's doctor eventually had to put her in the hospital for treatment. While there, she would secretly do all kinds of exercises, still hoping to lose more weight. After a number of hospitalizations and a lot of individual and family counseling, Heather was finally able to admit she had a problem and work to overcome it.

Common Symptoms of Eating Disorders

Symptoms (Note : Some people suffer from anorexia and bulimia and have symptoms of both disorders.)	Anorexia Nervosa	Bulimia Nervosa	Binge Eating Disorder
Excessive weight loss in relatively short period of time	✓		
Continuation of dieting although bone-thin	✓		
Dissatisfaction with appearance; belief that body is fat, even though body is severely underweight	✓		
Loss of monthly menstrual period	✓	✓	
Unusual interest in food and development of strange eating rituals	✓	✓	
Eating in secret	✓	✓	✓
Obsession with exercise	✓	✓	
Serious depression	✓	✓	✓
Bingeing—consuming large amounts of food		✓	✓
Vomiting or use of drugs to stimulate vomiting, bowel movements, and urination		✓	
Bingeing but no noticeable weight gain		✓	
Disappearence into bathroom for long periods of time to induce vomiting		✓	.
Abuse of drugs and/or alcohol		✓	✓

Source : National Institutes of Health.

Some doctors and scientists believe that bulimia may be more treatable than anorexia. It is not as easy to detect, however. People with anorexia are bone-thin, but those with bulimia maintain a much more normal appearance. As in the case of anorexia, early treatment of the illness is important.

Binge Eating Disorder

Binge eating disorder is similar to bulimia nervosa. Like bulimia, it is characterized by uncontrolled eating. However, people with this disorder do not purge their bodies of food after they have eaten. They keep on eating until they feel uncomfortably full, and they usually have more difficulty losing weight and keeping it off than others with obesity problems. About 2 percent of the population suffers from binge eating disorder, which is more common among women than men.

Since most people with binge eating disorder are overweight, they are likely to have the same medical problems that obesity brings—high blood pressure, high cholesterol, and diabetes.

Researchers at the National Institute of Mental Health have also found that many people with binge eating disorder suffer from depression. This depression may be related to any combination of problems associated with this disorder. Sufferers often hide their binge behavior by eating in secret and are then upset by their lack of self-control. Others turn to abusing drugs or alcohol, behavior known as trigger depression.

This colored scanning electron micrograph (SEM) shows the rod-shaped bacteria *Escherichia coli*—commonly called E. coli. E. coli bacteria are normal inhabitants of the human intestine but can increase in number and cause infection under certain conditions.

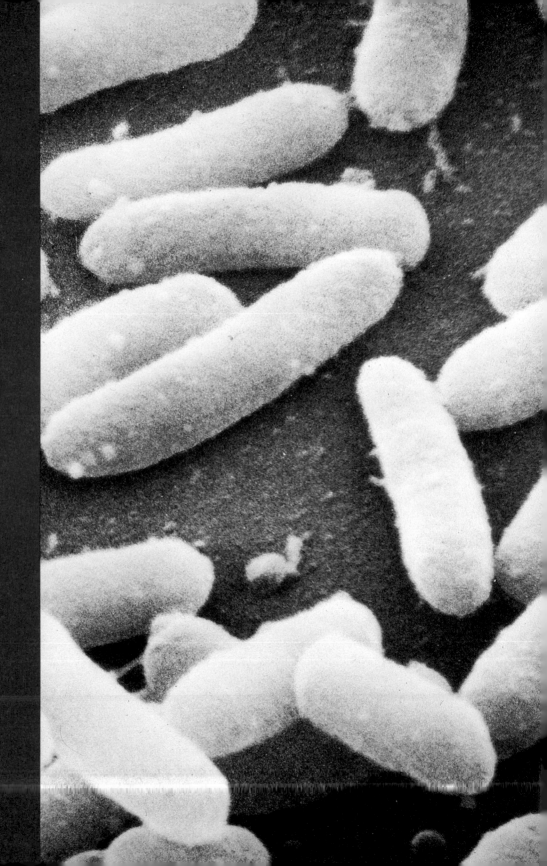

3

Digestive Diseases

In order for the body to take in nutrients from food, that food must be fully digested and absorbed. While digestion starts in the mouth and continues in the stomach, much work is left to be done in the small intestine (a 20-foot-long tube coiled in the abdomen).

Food enters the small intestine in a semiliquid form, where digestive juices assist in the final breakdown. Fully digested food is absorbed into the bloodstream through the lining of the small intestine, which is covered with villi. Villi are small projections that increase the surface area of the small intestine so that nutrients can be absorbed faster.

After the small intestine has absorbed the nutritional content of food, the semiliquid waste product passes to the large intestine, or colon. There, much of the water, salt, and other electrolytes (chemicals in body fluids, like sodium and potassium, that regulate such things as water balance) are reabsorbed into the body. This reabsorption is very important for good health, as the body needs constant and large amounts of water, as well as salt and electrolytes. The unabsorbed food and fibers are eliminated during a bowel movement. Diarrhea (watery bowel movements) left untreated can rapidly cause the body to lose its stores of water, salt, and other electrolytes.

Acute Gastrointestinal Illnesses
In many underdeveloped countries, so-called diarrheal diseases—infections of the gastrointestinal tract—are the leading causes of death among newborns and young children. In most of the industrialized world, including the United States, proper sanitation, good hygiene, and clean drinking water prevent large-scale epidemics of intestinal infections. However, the Centers for Disease Control estimate that each year about 25 million Americans, or 1 out of every 10 people, get a case of what is commonly called "a stomach bug."

About half of the intestinal infections are caused by viruses; the other half are caused by bacteria or parasites. The symptoms of an intestinal infection include watery diarrhea, possibly even with blood or mucus; cramping and abdominal pain; low-grade fever; nausea or vomiting or both; muscle aches; and headaches. Drinking lots of fluids and getting plenty of rest usually remedy the problem.

Water treatment facilities—like this one in Oakland, California—eliminate bacteria from our water supply. This is done by filtering the water to remove heavy metals and other substances and then adding oxygen to the water and exposing it to sunlight to kill any remaining bacteria.

For most people, gastrointestinal viruses are not dangerous. But they may be for young children, who can lose their body fluids very quickly, and for the elderly. They also endanger those whose immune systems (the body's disease-fighting system) are not functioning properly, including people who have AIDS or who are being treated with immunosuppressant drugs (drugs that reduce the activity of the body's immune system).

Gastrointestinal illnesses caused by bacteria are easier to identify than those caused by viruses. Most do not require any specific treatment. Some, however, will respond to antibiotics—drugs used to treat bacterial infections. Campylobacter, salmonella, and *Escherichia coli* are three bacteria that commonly cause gastrointestinal distress. When people eat food contaminated with these bacteria, they get what is often referred to as "food poisoning." The food—usually chicken, beef, or pork—becomes contaminated during processing. It is therefore important to cook these items sufficiently to kill the bacteria.

Parasitic gastrointestinal infections are relatively rare in the United States because of the clean public water supplies. However, people can get giardiasis, an infection caused by the *Giardia lamblia* parasite, by swimming in lakes or from the water in private wells.

Inflammatory Bowel Diseases
Inflammatory bowel diseases (ulcerative colitis and Crohn's disease) are characterized by inflammation of the intestine, which often leads to diarrhea, weight loss,

and malnutrition. Both diseases can strike at any time in life, although the peak age for diagnosis is between 15 and 30 years old.

When either disease begins in adolescence, it can have a severe impact on growth and development. For this reason, a prolonged bout with diarrhea, painful and urgent trips to the toilet, recurring low-grade fever, and flulike symptoms deserve the attention of a doctor, who may order a series of blood tests and other diagnostic procedures.

Ulcerative colitis is a condition in which raw, inflamed areas called ulcers, and small abscesses develop in the lining of the large intestine. The disease is not always active, but when it is, it causes a frequent need to empty the bowels; the bowel movements are often bloody.

Ulcerative colitis can be treated effectively with medications, including corticosteroids and immunosuppressant drugs. In extreme cases of the disease that do not respond to medical treatment, surgery is performed to remove the entire large intestine. In the past, this surgery almost always necessitated the creation of an opening in the lower abdomen to eliminate food wastes into a bag. (This procedure is called a colostomy.) However, surgical techniques introduced in the 1970s and perfected over the last two decades now allow most people to have the lower portion of the small intestine attached to the rectum (the muscle mass at the end of the intestine that releases waste through the anus and out of the body) and maintain relatively normal body function.

This X-ray shows the large intestine of a patient with Crohn's disease of the region where the large and small intestines join. Like ulcerative colitis, Crohn's disease is a chronic inflammatory disease, the cause of which is still unknown.

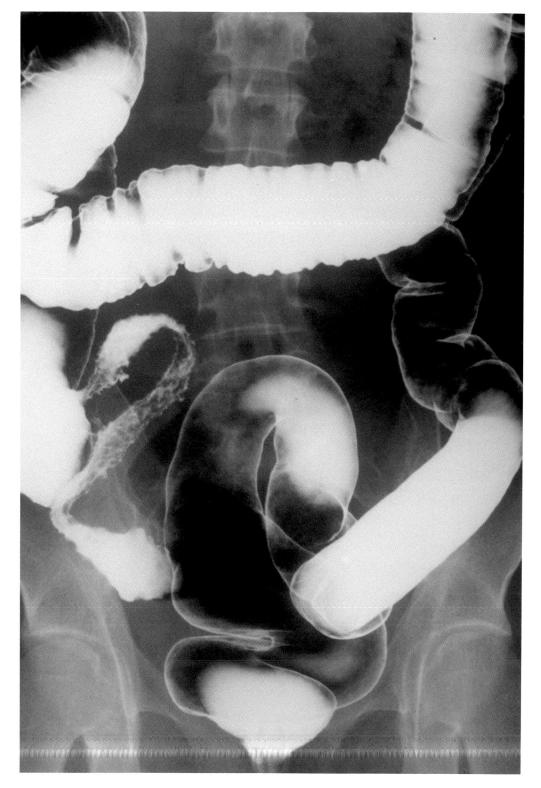

If a person has an especially severe flare-up of Crohn's disease, eating can become a chore, since it is often followed by discomfort, bloating, cramps, and diarrhea. Weight loss can occur quickly. Doctors frequently use high-calorie liquid dietary supplements to try to enhance nutrition. Sometimes they even administer liquid nutrients intravenously (through a vein in the arm) in order to give the intestines a complete rest.

Short-Gut Syndrome

While the large intestine is hardly ever removed in people with Crohn's disease, many Crohn's sufferers do need to have portions of their small intestine removed when it becomes narrowed and filled with scar tissue from repeated bouts with inflammation.

If enough of the small intestine is removed, it can lead to a condition called short-gut syndrome, which can cause malabsorption—the failure to absorb nutrients. Usually, if a small portion of the small intestine is removed, the rest of the organ can take over. However, in cases where many feet of the small intestine have been removed—especially toward the end of the organ—nutritional supplements may be necessary to counteract malabsorption.

Short-gut syndrome can also occur in people born without a normal-sized or fully formed small intestine, but this is very rare.

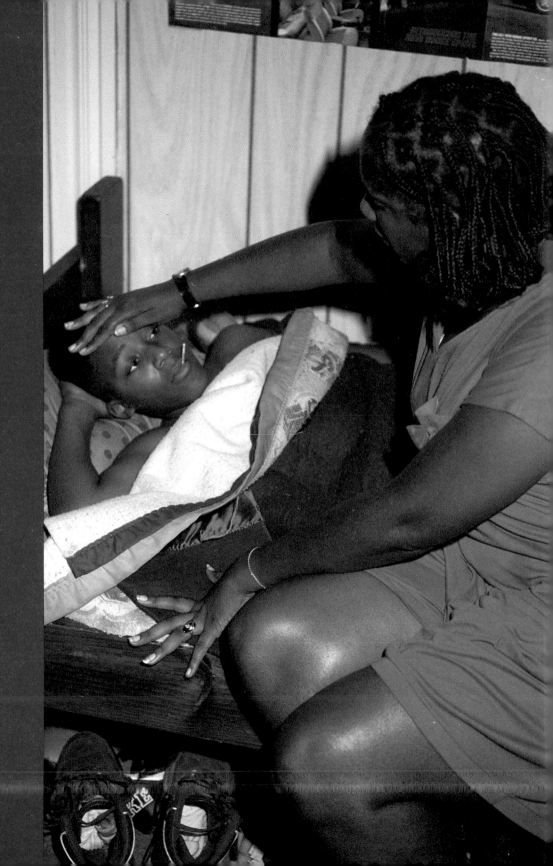

Some nutritional disorders are detected at birth, while others do not develop until later in life. Celiac disease usually begins during childhood and can initially appear to be a simple stomach virus. However, celiac disease is caused by an inability to tolerate the protein found in wheat and rye.

4

Metabolic Disorders and Food Allergies

Some nutritional problems are caused by genetic defects that are responsible for a wide variety of severe illnesses. Others, known as food allergies, are caused by adverse reactions to food, which can be prevented through avoidance of the offending food.

Metabolic Disorders
The chemical reactions that allow the body to turn food into energy and allow the organs and tissues to perform their proper functions are known as metabolism. The chemical reactions that are responsible for metabolism are called metabolic pathways.

Medical researchers have described hundreds of metabolic pathways. A mistake in a single step of just one of these pathways can cause a series of major problems. These genetic mistakes are called inborn errors of metabolism. While some of these errors can be corrected by use of a specially made baby formula (medical food), others require more complicated treatment. The most severe of these metabolic diseases lead to death in infancy or childhood.

Even some of the babies whose diseases are detected very early will have been damaged enough that they suffer from seizures; mental retardation; or problems with walking, talking, seeing, or hearing. Most inborn errors of metabolism are diagnosed by blood tests that can show which metabolic pathway is not functioning properly. Because of this, each state in the country has a blood-testing program for newborn babies that is designed to detect the most common inborn errors of metabolism. If an affected baby can be identified in the first few weeks of life, and if the inborn error of metabolism is the kind that can be controlled by a special baby formula, he or she can often escape the damaging effects to the brain.

Many metabolic diseases are seen in generation after generation of a family. By having a blood test, adults can find out if they are carriers of the gene for a particular metabolic disease. Carriers are people who have inherited from one of their parents the ability to pass on a disease to their own children but who do not actually have the disease themselves. If a man and a woman both carry the gene for a metabolic disease, they may choose not to have children to avoid passing on a serious disease to another generation.

Phenylketonuria (PKU) is probably the best understood inborn error of metabolism. It occurs in about 1 out of every 16,000 babies born in the United States.

Babies born with PKU are missing an enzyme (a protein that makes chemical reactions more efficient) called phenylalanine hydroxylase. This enzyme is used by the body to metabolize (break down) the amino acid phenylalnine into smaller chemical parts.

When a baby with PKU is fed a standard infant formula or breast milk, and the body digests the proteins in the formula or breast milk, all the amino acids can be used for energy except the phenylalanine. Since the body is unable to do anything with the phenylalanine, it builds up to abnormally high levels in the blood. If not discovered soon enough, this buildup can cause mental retardation, seizures, microcephaly (an abnormally small head size), a musty smell to the body, and various other abnormalities.

Fortunately, all babies in the United States are tested for PKU shortly after birth, and there is a special baby formula made without phenylalanine that allows babies with PKU to develop normally.

When a child with PKU is ready to eat solid foods, the amounts and types of food he or she is allowed to eat are restricted and closely watched so that the amount of phenylalanine in the blood stays low. Most of the foods we eat are fairly high in phenylalanine.

The older a child gets, the more difficult it becomes to stay on the PKU-restricted diet. Most children find it boring to eat a limited number of foods, and the special

Genetic counseling is an option that some people choose either before they decide to have a baby or after they have had a baby who has a metabolic disorder. This type of counseling helps parents decide what course of action is best for their specific situation.

formula for older children and adults does not have a particularly nice taste. Unfortunately, people with PKU must watch their phenylalanine intake all their lives and should continue to supplement their diet with medical food in order to remain healthy.

It is especially important for women with PKU to be on an extremely rigid diet when they are expecting a baby—even during the months when they are trying to become pregnant—so that the unborn child is able to develop inside a normal body with a normal level of phenylalanine.

Maple syrup urine disease (MSUD) is another disorder of amino acid metabolism. It acquired its name because the urine, sweat, and earwax of babies with the condition smell like burnt sugar or maple syrup. About half the states in the country routinely test newborns for MSUD. It is seen in 1 in 250,000 babies born in the United States.

MSUD occurs when the body is unable to break down a group of amino acids called the branched-chain amino acids because it can't make a substance called thiamine pyrophosphate. The levels of the branched-chain amino acids in the blood become abnormally high, causing vomiting, poor feeding, rigid muscles, and seizures. The condition can be fatal or nearly fatal to newborns.

When a baby with MSUD is fed a specially prepared formula, the amino acid levels decrease and the baby can usually develop normally. People with MSUD must remain on a low-protein diet, supplemented by special medical food all their lives, or dizziness, extreme tiredness, coma, and death can occur at any time.

Galactosemia is the inability of the body to break down galactose (a type of carbohydrate found in the natural sugar in cow's milk, breast milk, and milk-based baby formulas) into glucose. This inability is due to the absence of an enzyme in the liver.

More than half of the states in the country test newborns for galactosemia. It is found in 1 out of every 50,000 to 60,000 newborns and can occur in all ethnic groups.

Galactosemia does not cause any symptoms at birth. Soon after, however, babies with galactosemia develop vomiting, diarrhea, and seizures, and they fail to gain weight. Their brain and liver can be severely damaged and they can develop cataracts. (A cataract is a film over the eye that can cause blindness.)

Treatment involves a diet free of galactose, which means that only lactose-free milk can be drunk. Thus, if treatment is started early, babies with galactosemia will develop normally. Untreated babies will die from malnutrition, liver damage, and infection.

Tay-Sachs disease (TSD) is caused by the accumulation of lipids (fats) in brain cells and prevents normal brain function. Children with TSD are missing a substance called hexosaminidase A. Lipids slowly collect in the cells of the brain and the eye, causing permanent damage.

Babies with TSD appear normal at birth, but at two to six months, signs of an abnormal nervous system begin to develop—tight muscles, seizures, the inability to eat, and an unusual sensitivity to noise. Children with TSD usually do not live beyond five years of age.

Food Allergies

People of all ages can have a variety of bad reactions to foods. Some adverse reactions are known as true food allergies, while others are called food intolerances. In true food allergy, the bad reaction is controlled by the immune system and can involve the skin, the respiratory tract, and the cardiovascular system (the system

A father feeds his child medical food (specially prepared formula) to combat the infant's inability to break down branched-chain amino acids. Several metabolic disorders are due to the body's inability to process specific types of amino acids.

involving the heart and blood vessels). Responses can range from severe skin rashes to wheezing and, sometimes, even death. Food intolerance, on the other hand, is more likely to involve the skin or the gastrointestinal tract, with reactions such as mild skin rashes or vomiting and diarrhea.

The impact of a true food allergy or a food intolerance on a person's overall nutrition is not usually severe. The food allergy or intolerance is generally limited to a narrow range of foods. There are often a number of substitutes for these foods that can help achieve a balanced diet.

Lactose intolerance occurs among people who are unable to digest lactose, a sugar found in cow's milk. This inability is caused by the absence, or near absence, of the enzyme produced in the small intestine that breaks down lactose. When a lactose-intolerant individual drinks milk or eats a food containing milk or another dairy product, such as cheese or ice cream, he or she will experience abdominal cramps and diarrhea, which may be mild or severe.

Some lactose-intolerant people are able to eat dairy products if they take a pill containing the enzyme they lack. Others, however, are unable to eat dairy products under any circumstances. Babies with lactose intolerance are often given soybean-based formulas, which do not contain lactose. Lactose intolerance can begin in childhood, adolescence, or adulthood.

Celiac disease, also known as celiac sprue, occurs in individuals who are unable to tolerate gluten, a protein

Lactose intolerance is a common food allergy. Medications and specially treated dairy products, however, are widely available, enabling many lactose-intolerant people to consume milk products.

found in the grains wheat and rye. Celiac disease is usually treated easily with a gluten-free diet.

This disease, which is not common, generally starts in childhood. The gluten damages the lining of the small intestine, causing diarrhea, irritability, vomiting, weight loss, and vitamin and mineral deficiencies. Unless foods containing wheat or rye are eliminated from the diet, the condition will get worse. Occasionally, the symptoms do not develop until adolescence or adulthood. In some individuals, the disease is so mild that symptoms never develop.

True food allergies are most commonly caused by foods such as fish, peanuts, eggs, milk, and soy. In the allergic, these foods can produce skin rashes like hives and eczema; severe vomiting and diarrhea; swelling of the lips, tongue, or throat; and wheezing. They can also cause a severe allergic reaction called anaphylaxis, which usually includes swelling of the respiratory tract, hives, and a drop in blood pressure that can be fatal. It has been shown that, among foods, peanuts are the most likely to cause life-threatening reactions.

An unusual form of food allergy is called food-associated exercise-induced anaphylaxis. People affected by this type of allergic reaction will suffer from hives, wheezing, or anaphylaxis if they eat a certain food and then exercise vigorously. The most commonly involved foods are celery, peaches, and shellfish.

The best way to prevent a recurrence of an allergic reaction is to avoid the food (and any related products) that has caused the reaction in the past. A person with

The foods shown here can cause life-threatening allergic reactions in people who have true food allergies.

severe allergies should always read the list of ingredients on the labels of prepared foods before buying them and should ask about how foods have been prepared in cafeterias or restaurants.

For people who have had severe reactions to foods in the past, doctors prescribe an injectable form of epinephrine that patients are told to carry with them at all times. Use of this drug at the first sign of a food reaction can save the allergic person from anaphylaxis and sudden death.

At a World Vision feeding center in Somalia, malnourished Somalis are given desperately needed food. Vitamins are also provided to help prevent disease.

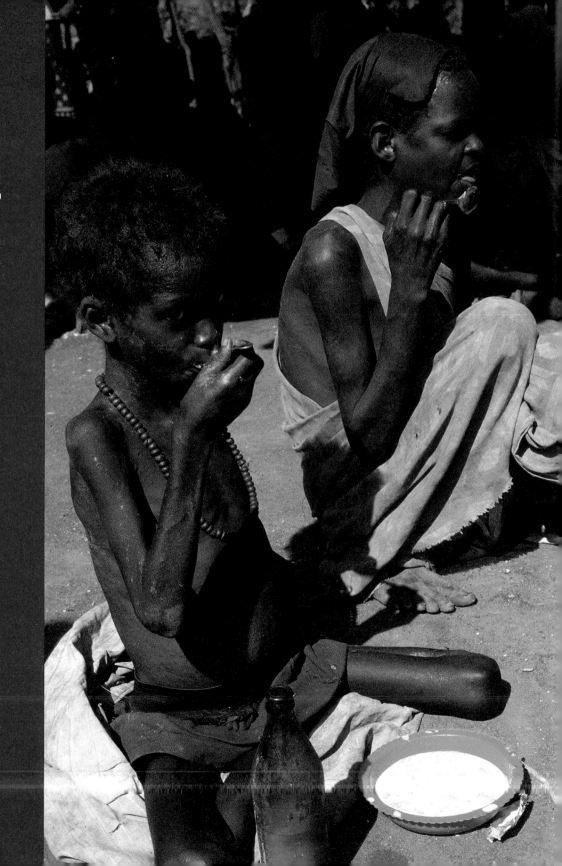

5

Hope and Help for Nutritional Problems

From laboratories to doctors' offices and hospitals, to the halls of Congress and the World Health Organization, scientists, medical personnel, and government officials continue to study the connections between nutrition and disease from a number of different angles.

Getting Food to the Malnourished
Nationally and internationally there are efforts to get food to people in need and to create and distribute inexpensive dietary supplements that can put an end to the diseases caused by malnutrition. Scientists are working to identify and develop treatments for diseases that cause malnutrition or the inability to digest important nutrients. Some researchers are even trying to determine whether diets that are rich in particular nutrients can ward off disease.

Somalis aid in the effort to deliver food to the starving people of their country.

As a matter of public policy, the federal government and most states do all they can to help Americans, especially the poor who live in rural and inner-city areas, receive adequate nutrition. They do this through programs such as Women, Infants and Children (WIC), which provides free food as well as nutritional counseling to many poor, pregnant women and mothers of infants and toddlers. Some state and local governments occasionally distribute surplus food to families and individuals.

Public-health and nutrition experts continue to look for ways to create programs in underdeveloped countries. The number of people at risk for diseases related to malnutrition is so great in these areas, however, that it is difficult to deal with the problem successfully.

Administering Food Supplements

In famine-stricken Somalia in 1993, World Health Organization officials did organize Somalian health workers to administer one large dose of Vitamin A to each malnourished child. Since the 1960s, Vitamin A supplements have been used in malnourished children to prevent xerophthalmia, a Vitamin A deficiency that can cause severe damage to the eyes and even blindness. A number of studies by public-health officials around the world in the early 1990s showed that a single high dose of Vitamin A could actually reduce the death rate among malnourished children from such infectious diseases as measles, diarrhea, dysentery, and simple respiratory infections.

Tests for metabolic diseases that keep people from digesting important food elements are continually being refined. In addition, the supplements taken by people with such conditions are being enhanced.

Using Drugs to Combat Digestive Diseases

Medical problems are widespread in patients with inflammatory bowel diseases (IBD), namely ulcerative colitis and Crohn's disease. In addition to aggressive nutritional support (mentioned in Chapter 3), medications are used both to ease the symptoms and temporarily stop the inflammatory process. A cure will be possible only when the causes of IBD are discovered.

The main theory today is that people with IBD have immune systems that actually fight their own bodies. Such a condition is known as an autoimmune disease. There are scientists who believe a common virus that most people fight off remains in the body of some people and from time to time flares up, causing the immune system to work to fight off the virus. Even when the immune system has beaten back the virus, it continues to act as if there were a problem and causes damage to various parts of the body.

Doctors who treat people with IBD use a combination of immunosuppressant drugs and other drugs. The immunosuppressants quiet down the reaction of the immune system. The problem with using immunosuppressants is that they leave people with a weakened immune system and they are susceptible to infections and illnesses.

Many young people are afflicted with inflammatory bowel disease. They are frequently given immunosuppressant drugs during severe flare-ups.

In the past, immunosuppressants have been the "last hope" of people with severe inflammatory bowel disease. In the future, low doses that act as "immuno-regulators" may be the first line of attack against the disease. By putting a patient's immune system back on track, doctors may be able to stem the course of inflammatory bowel disease, which today is a constant series of flare-ups and calm periods.

Dealing with Eating Disorders

While inflammatory bowel diseases and metabolic diseases have presented quite a challenge to the medical community, fighting eating disorders, which affect so many teenagers, will be even more difficult. That is because eating disorders have both physical and psychological components that require intensive treatment over a long period of time. A keen awareness of the problem and the increase in the number of clinics and individuals experienced in treating these disorders, however, have brightened the picture considerably. In addition, the National Institute of Mental Health is funding the work of research scientists who are studying ways to treat and understand eating disorders. This work holds great promise for the future.

The Role of Nutrition in Genetic Diseases

In May of 1993, a number of scientists gathered at the National Institutes of Health outside Washington, D.C., for a conference to mark the beginning of a new project: the "Bionutrition Initiative." This was an attempt to see if scientists can find enough genetic clues to diseases, such as cancer and heart disease, to enable doctors and nutritionists to prescribe the proper diet to lessen their patients' risk factors.

For instance, if genetic markers for heart disease could be found, a person would know as a child that he or she had a higher chance of getting heart disease than a person without the genetic marker present—40 or 50 years before any symptoms might begin to show up.

Thus, early on, doctors and nutritionists might be able to prescribe diets low in saturated fats (butter and margarine, for example). While children with high cholesterol levels are already put on such diets, finding a genetic marker would allow these children to be treated even if they had no outward signs of possible heart disease.

Where to Find Help
There is help for everyone who is suffering from a nutritional problem, whether it be obesity, anorexia, bulimia, a digestive disease, or a food allergy. Listed here are the names of some national organizations that can help. They can supply information on specific problems and can provide the names of sources to contact for advice and treatment.

American Anorexia/Bulimia Association, Inc.
(AABA)
418 East 76th Street
New York, NY 10021
(212) 734-1114

Anorexia Nervosa and Related Eating Disorders, Inc.
(ANRED)
P.O. Box 5102
Eugene, OR 97405
(503) 344-1144

Asthma and Allergy Foundation of America
1125 15th Street, N.W.
Washington, D.C. 20005
(800) 727-8462

Bulimia Anorexia Self Help, Inc.
(BASH)
6125 Clayton Avenue, Suite 215
St. Louis, MO 63139
(314) 567-4080

Center for the Study of Anorexia and Bulimia
1 West 91st Street
New York, NY 10024
(212) 595-3449

Crohns and Colitis Foundation of America, Inc.
444 Park Avenue South
New York, NY 10016
(800) 932-2423

Food and Nutrition Information and Education
    Resources Center, Room 304
National Agricultural Library Building
10301 Baltimore Blvd.
Beltsville, MD 20705
(301) 344-3719

Foundation for Education About Eating Disorders
(FEED)
P.O. Box 16375
Baltimore, MD 21210
(410) 467-0603

National Anorexic Aid Society (NAAS)
Harding Hospital
1925 East Dublin Granville Road
Columbus, OH 43229
(614) 436-1112

National Association to Advance Fat Acceptance
(NAAFA)
Box 188620
Sacramento, CA 95818
(800) 442-1214

National Association of Anorexia Nervosa and
     Associated Disorders (ANAD)
P.O. Box 7
Highland Park, IL 60035
(708) 831-3438

National Digestive Diseases Education and
     Information Clearinghouse
1555 Wilson Blvd., Suite 600
Rosslyn, VA 22209
(703) 496-9707

Overeaters Anonymous (OA)
P.O. Box 92870
Los Angeles, CA 90009
(310) 618-8835

Glossary

amenorrhea The absence of monthly menstrual periods.

amino acids The building blocks of proteins, some of which are found in foods, others of which are made by the body.

anaphylaxis A life-threatening allergic reaction.

anorexia nervosa An eating disorder in which a person refuses to eat sufficient quantities of food and loses too much weight.

antibiotics Drugs that help the body fight infections caused by bacteria.

bacteria One-celled, microscopic organisms, some of which cause infection.

bradycardia An abnormally slow heart rate—below 60 beats per minute.

bulimia nervosa An eating disorder in which a person eats large amounts of food and then tries to rid the body of them by methods such as self-induced vomiting and the abuse of laxatives.

calorie A unit that measures the energy-producing value of food.

carbohydrates Sugars, starches, and cellulose, the compounds made up of oxygen, hydrogen, and carbon only.

cardiovascular system The system involving the heart and blood vessels.

cholesterol A type of fat found in animal tissues and foods derived from animal fats.

constipation Bowel movements that are hard, infrequent, and difficult to pass from the body.

coronary arteries The blood vessels that supply freshly oxygenated blood to the heart muscle.

diarrhea Frequent watery bowel movements.

electrolyte A substance that can conduct electricity when in solution. The major blood electrolytes are sodium, potassium, chloride, and bicarbonate.

endocrine system The collection of ductless glands in the body—thyroid, adrenals, ovaries (in the female) and testes (in the male), and a portion of the pancreas that produce hormones.

enzyme A substance that makes chemical reactions more efficient.

esophagitis Inflammation and irritation of the esophagus.

fat A combination of fatty acids and other substances found in animal tissue, seeds, nuts, and fruits.

fatty acids Substances containing carbon, hydrogen, and oxygen that are found in fats.

fermentation A chemical reaction that breaks down complex carbohydrates into simple carbohydrates.

food allergy An unusual reaction of the body to a specific food.

gastrointestinal tract The pathway that connects the mouth to the anus, consisting of the mouth, throat, esophagus, stomach, small intestine, and large intestine.

hormone A chemical formed by one organ of the body and then carried by the blood to another organ to help the second organ function.

hypotension Abnormally low blood pressure.

hypothermia Abnormally low body temperature—below 95°F. (35°C.).

immune system The parts of the body that protect it against infections and infectious diseases. When the immune system turns on the body itself, it is known as an autoimmune condition.

immunosuppressant A drug or other substance that reduces or eliminates immune-system function. Immunosupressant drugs are given to keep the immune system from turning on the body or from rejecting a transplanted organ, such as a heart.

lactase The enzyme that breaks down lactose, the sugar molecule in milk.

lactose One of the sugars present in milk.

lactose intolerance The inability of the small intestine to absorb lactose.

laxative A medication that causes soft, and sometimes frequent, bowel movements.

lipids Fatty substances, including cholesterol, present in blood and body tissues.

malabsorption The inability of the small intestine to efficiently use the food that passes through it, normally a result of infection, injury, or a metabolic disease.

malnutrition Undernutrition due to lack of food, disease, or both.

metabolism Chemical reactions that allow the body to function properly.

minerals Chemical substances that are neither animal nor vegetable, some of which are necessary for the function of the human body.

nutrient A component of a food or other substance used for the growth and nourishment of a living organism.

nutrition The use of food by a person, animal, or other living thing for growth.

obesity A condition in which there is too much body fat.

parasite An organism that depends on another organism for nourishment and protection.

protein A substance made up of a chain of amino acids, present in all living tissue and necessary for growth and cell repair.

puberty The stage of development during which a person becomes physically mature enough to have children.

purge To empty, clean, or purify; in the medical sense, usually the emptying of the bowels; in the case of eating disorders, to empty the stomach.

saturated fats Fats, such as butter and margarine, that are solid at room temperature.

vegetarian A person who does not eat foods derived from animals.

villi Tiny outpouchings of tissue that make up the inner surface of the gastrointestinal tract, allowing the small intestine to absorb nutrients faster.

virus The smallest known type of infectious agent.

Further Reading

Franz, William, and Franz, Barbara. *Nutritional Survival Manual for the 80s: A Young People's Guide and Dietary Goals for the U.S.* New York: Simon & Schuster, 1981.

Kubersky, Rachel. *Everything You Need to Know About Eating Disorders.* New York: The Rosen Publishing Group, 1992.

Maloney, Michael, M.D., and Kramer, Rachel. *Straight Talk About Eating Disorders.* New York: Facts On File, 1991.

McCoy, Kathy, and Wibbelsman, Charles, M.D. *The New Teenage Body Book.* New York: Body Press, 1992.

Moe, Barbara. *Coping with Eating Disorders.* New York: The Rosen Publishing Group, 1991.

National Foundation for Ileitis & Colitis (now called National Crohn's & Colitis Foundation). *The Crohn's Disease and Ulcerative Colitis Fact Book.* New York: Scribners, 1983.

Silverstein, Alvin, Silverstein, Virginia, and Silverstein, Robert. *So You Think You're Fat?* New York: HarperCollins, 1991.

Index

Photo Credits:

Page 4: ©Lee Snyder/Photo Researchers, Inc.; pp. 6, 18: ©Mary Lauzon; p. 8:
©Margaret Miller/Photo Researchers, Inc.; p. 10: ©Richard Hutchings/Photo
Researchers, Inc.; p. 21: ©Catherine Ursillo/Photo Researchers, Inc.; pp. 23, 42:
©Will and Deni McIntyre/Photo Researchers, Inc.; p. 25: ©Blackbirch Graphics; pp.
28, 34, 36: ©Photo Researchers, Inc.; p. 31: ©Lawrence Migdale/Photo Researchers,
Inc.; pp. 38, 47, 55: ©Stuart Rabinowitz; p. 45: ©J. Gerard Smith/Photo Researchers,
Inc.; p. 49: ©Richard Hutchings/Photo Researchers, Inc.; p. 50: ©Bruce Brander/Photo
Researchers, Inc., p.52. ©Duclos/Van Der Stockt/Gamma Liaison.